MW00745066

Ex Libris
C. K. OGDEN

CONTENTIONS WITH GOD

A STUDY IN JEWISH FOLK-LORE

BY

Dr. IMMANUEL OLŜVANGER.

PUBLISHED
under the auspices of the
Cape Town Jewish Historical and Literary Society
BY
T. MASKEW MILLER, CAPE TOWN.
"HASEFFR"

Digitized for Microsoft Corporation
by the Internet Archive in 2007
From University of California Libraries
May be used for non-commercial, personal, research,
or educational purposes, or any fair use
May not be indexed in a commercial service.

BM
530
O4

LIBRARY
UNIVERSITY OF CALIFORNIA
SANTA BARBARA

To Prof. Dr. Ed. Hoffmann-Krayer, Basle,
Chairman of the Swiss Society for Folk-lore
this essay is respectfully and gratefully
dedicated.

My dear Professor,

Since the occasion some two years ago, when I had the honour to deliver a lecture under the same title as this essay to the Basle Section of the Swiss Society for Folk-lore I have not ceased to prosecute my humble investigations further in this field   In the trust that the publication of the results of my own inquiries may stimulate others with wider knowledge and greater ability to carry the subject further, I have ventured to publish this essay, and in this I have been encouraged both by Israel Zangwill's and your own friendly criticism of my book "Rosinkess mit Mandlen."

Moreover I feel sure that you will deal kindly with any errors which may appear to your scientific eye, more especially in some story or other which you may consider to be not altogether germane to the title.   Yet are they undoubtedly cognate to the subject; and therefore they are included,-to use a word of Ariosto,- *per raccontar piacevole a ricreazione delle persone d'animo gentile.* And even though I am keenly aware that my tales are not nearly so *piacevole* told as those of Ariosto, yet I believe that the *animo gentile* of the reader will see beauty even in those stories which may be rejected by the vulgus.

In reading some grotesque anecdote you will with your deeper understanding not find it to accuse: " How impious is this people who, even when speaking of God, sees fit to jest "

Rather will you see reality like the Chassidic Rabbi Lebi-Isaak Berditschewer, about whom it is told, that once, while walking with a friend, he came across a Jewish cabdriver, in Praying Shawl and Phylacteries greasing the axles of a waggon. " What an uncouth man this is!" exclaimed the friend, "even while he prays, he greases the axles." For a moment the Rabbi thought, then turning to his friend he said : "What a truly pious man this is! even while he greases the axles, he prays."

With these remarks I offer, not without some feeling of trepidation, this essay to you.

With affectionate greetings,

Yours very sincerely

Dr Immanuel Olsvanger

C.T. 1921.

I wish to express indebtedness to my friend Mr. S. Turtledove of Cape Town for rendering me invaluable assistance with the English MS.

. . . tutti fanno bello il primo giro,
E differentemente han dolce vita,
Per sentir più e men l'Eterno Spiro.

(Dante. Paradiso IV 34—36)

THE following essay attempts to make a survey of the realm of Jewish folk-lore, in particular of that section of folk-lore which concerns itself with the relations existing between Man and his Maker.

Before actually discussing the subject, we would introduce our readers into the milieu of Jewish folk-life. Let us take, for example, a small Jewish township in Lithuania or Poland. The inhabitants of the place are poor, tired "Luftmenschen" who do not know from one day to another whence will come their daily bread. They are hated and mocked at by the natives; anxiety for the provision of their large families, aye, for the preservation of very life itself, consumes them body and soul. But if one desires to probe what sways the innermost feelings of the hearts of these persecuted and downtrodden unfortunates, then one should take a point of vantage, before sunrise, in one of the streets of the township on the Penitential Days between New Year and the Day of Atonement. The narrow street is dimly lit by a feeble oil-lamp. The worthy citizens are still in their beds, and the shutters of the small, low, wooden houses are not yet opened. But on the street corner, there where the Synagogue stands at the crossing, appears the bent figure of an old Jew enveloped in a shabby fur coat with his collar above his ears, a small lantern in one hand and a thick staff in the other; he is the beadle of the Synagogue. As he goes from house to house, he knocks with his stick at each window, for it is time to arouse the sleepers for early morning worship. And as he makes his round, thus he chants his simple and soul-moving tune :

> Arise, ye Jews, dear pious Jews!
> Arise for the praise of the Creator !
> The God is in exile,
> God's Soul is in exile,
> The People is in exile !
> Arise, arise, to praise the Creator !

This simple melody opens to one's spiritual eyes the profoundest depths of the Jewish folk-soul. The nation would surely have found it impossible to endure the severe sufferings of the centuries of exile, had she not the joy-bringing consciousness that her God had not abandoned her. For so did God love His People that He followed them into exile. When the Temple was razed to the ground, the Ancient of Days covered His countenance and vowed to accompany them whithersoever they wandered, relates an old legend of the nation. And legend is the highest expression of truth, more genuine than the truth of history, for while the latter must be demonstrated and proved, must be studied and can be forgotten, the former lives deep in the consciousness of the race.

To free God and himself from exile is the task of the Jew in his life of suffering.

The suffering of the nation is shared by God who is in exile with her. In this Divine co-suffering the sublime greatness of God's love manifests itself. It is the love of the God who constantly dwells (*shokhen*) amongst His children. Therefore the people attributes to Him the name "*Shekhinah*" which designation and the way it is conceived by the people is somewhat expressive of maternal love and compassion. In other languages we could hardly find any adequate translation of this term and all that it implies. One might translate it into "God's Soul" or "the God-Mother," i.e. God in his motherly relations to His children.

The Shekhinah, the God-Mother, lavishes an endless love on Israel, and is her Pillar of Cloud and Pillar of Fire.

On handing over the Torah, the Holy Doctrine, to the People, God said, "Behold! in that ye have said, 'Hear, O Israel, the Lord is One', ye have made Me the only Treasure in the world, and I too will make ye an only treasure in the world, in that I say, 'Who is like unto Thy People Israel, an only nation on the earth" (Berachoth, 6). God made an eternal covenant of love with His People; and as a perpetual reminder of this bond the Jews put on daily the phylacteries containing a parchment scroll, on which is written the dogma, "Hear O Israel!"

God too, it is said, puts on similar phylacteries, and in His are written the words, "Who is like unto Thy People Israel, an only nation on the earth" (Sanhedrin 7,14).

God and People—for both this rite is a bounden duty. Through it is maintained the eternal Unity of which the Zohar speaks, "The Holy One, blessed be He, Israel, and the Torah, all these are an indivisible Unity" Thus runs the dogma of. Trinity of the Jewish religion. The real connecting link of these three component parts of this Trinity is the Torah, which opens to the people the way of a righteous life. Right and Righteousness form the quintessential content of the Divine Teaching. "He who does Right, becomes united with God."

In a Midrash are quoted the following words of God: "Of all peoples I loved Israel, of all my creations—Right: accordmgly, I give My beloved creation to My beloved people! Israel, m that ye do Right, am *I* exalted" (Deuteronomy Raba 5).

It is for God to cause Right and Righteousness to reign in the life of man; and His nation is to be of service to Him in the fulfilment of this task. If a man performs the duty of an upright judge even for one hour, the Talmud says of him, that, together with God, he is a *concreator of the world*. And God, the Dispenser of Justice, does not judge according to His own opinion alone, but He causes the whole Heavenly Host to appear before His Throne, and invites the opinion of each of them (Jer. Sanhedrin 1; Tanchuma Exodus).

Indeed, not only does He solicit the opinions of the angels, but He receives with due consideration the views of his People, Israel On one occasion, when one of the Rabbis of the Talmud encountered the prophet Elijah, he asked the prophet: "What does God do?" The prophet replied: "God deliberates on the verdicts of wise men" (Chaggiga 15). So closely is God bound with His people. What is holy for the nation according to divine command, is also holy for the Giver of that command—the Temple and its vessels, the Torah and its guardians on earth, the priests.

During the festival service on a certain Day of Atonement God even appeared in the Holy of Holies to the High Priest Ismael and said to him: "Ismael, My son, bless Me". The priest said: "Lord of the Universe, may Thy mercy overcome Thine anger"

And the Lord of the Universe with a friendly nod of His head showd that He was pleased with the benediction of the priest. From this the Talmud adopts the moral: "May the blessing of an inferior not be negligeable in your sight" (Berakhoth 6). A benediction from whomsoever it may proceed, is always of great importance for the future of its recipient.

In the dawn of Jewish history, the progenitor of the race, Jacob, had to struggle with God before he could obtain His benediction. Only after a combat lasting a whole night, a combat in which God was vanquished by the man Jacob, did the Lord of the Universe consider Himself compelled to bless the patriarch, and He named him Israel, the God-fighter.* In combat with God, Jacob won an eternal spiritual bond and a bond of love with Him. That is the inner meaning of the Jacob story. It certainly has a ring of the old fables of the battles of the gods, with which all cosmogonical myths associate the beginning of the world. What, however, distinguishes our legend from the others, is that it concerns itself in our case with the struggle between God and the *man* Jacob, while the Theomachy of the others relates the struggles of the gods among themselves or with their enemies the demons (the latter being a development of the former).

Certain authorities (Gressman, Eduard Meyer, Wundt and others) hold that this legend in its original form makes Jacob to fight not with God, but with a river demon, who was obstructing his passage, and who, according to the usage of these spirits, left the field at day-break. They may be right, they may be wrong. Be that as it may, it is impossible to adduce definite proof either way. To determine the original form of this legend is, after all, only of value to the history of literature; in the investigation of the Jewish folk-soul it is absolutely immaterial, because the version which has it that her progenitor actually fought with God and conquered Him, holds a position of profound and indisputable truth in the belief of the nation.

---

* We can differ as to whether the teller of the story makes Jacob fight with God or with an angel. True, the Talmud explains it in the latter sense (Chulin 92) But the narrator puts at the end of the story, the following words in the mouth of Jacob "I have seen Elohim face to face". Here Elohim can hardly have any other meaning but God.

The conception, that God can be vanquished in a struggle with man, does not occur with an equal boldness amongst any other race.

The ancient Indians were, it is true, in doubt concerning God's all-embracing knowledge and wisdom. The God of Death, Yama, when asked by the poor youth Naciketas, who was sacrificed to the god in the manner of the daughter of Jephtah, refuses at the beginning to offer any enlightenment on the ultimate questions of life. And who does not know the famous Hymn of the Veda, 'the hymn of that religious atheism which alone can bring out real religion'?

> Who knows the secret? who proclaimed it here?
> Whence, whence this manifold creation sprang?
> The Gods themselves came later into being,
> Who knows from whence this great creation sprang?
> He from whom all this great creation came,
> Whether his will created or was mute,
> The most high Seer, that is in the highest heaven,
> He knows it! or perchance even He knows not?

But never would the singer of this or similar hymns express the thought, that the Creator could accept advice from, or be taught by a man.

According to an ancient Jewish conception, wisdom is not an attribute of God, but rather a spring which has a separate existence, and to which God himself alone first perceived the way. Thus says Job in one of his speeches.

> Whence comes wisdom?
> Where is the place of understanding?
> Only God knew the way to it and knew its place.
> He saw it and revealed it,
> He prepared it and probed it,
> And He said to man:
> "Behold, the Fear of God—that is Wisdom."

Wisdom, consequently, existed independently of God, God had to find the way to it, and fathom it previous to revealing it to man Characteristically the Rabbis infer from this the rule . "First consider deliberately, then, having acquired a firm grasp of the subject and complete clearness, speak, because thuswise did God with wisdom" (Exodus Raba 40; Tanchuma Jethro).

In consequence, by revealing Wisdom to His people through the Torah, which itself drained the source of Wisdom dry, God made that Wisdom as equally accessible to man as to Himself. Thus man is, as it were, put on an equal footing with God, and can, by means of his human reasoning, seek to influence Him.

It often occurs in the Bible that God is restrained by pious patriarchs or elders of the tribe from carrying out severe penalties. We are reminded of how Abraham in a long discussion, which forms one of the finest passages of the Scriptures, sought to save the cities of Sodom and Gomorrah. He succeeds in obtaining an undertaking from God to show mercy, if there should be found in those cities even ten pious men In reading the dialogue one invariably receives the impression, that nothing would have been more pleasing to God than to have been able to grant Abraham's humane request.

He is always ready to receive sincere repentance, as is seen in the case of Nineveh, when Jonah urges God to keep His pledged word and to destroy the city; God causes him to experience the miracle of the gourd, described in a story which speaks in earnest and childlike tones to the heart of every man Jonah's contention (the whole Jonah-narrative being, in my opinion, constructed as a parallel to the previously mentioned story of Abraham) is rejected by God, not because of His superior power, but by the force of impartial Right.

When God destroyed the Temple, Abraham rose up as a complainant against Him and found strong support among the angels. "What is it that Israel has done?" he demanded of God. "Who shall be witness that she transgressed the Torah?" And God answered that the Torah herself would bear testimony to that effect. But when the Torah, obeying God's summons, appeared, Abraham reproached her, saying, "My daughter, dost thou forget how, when God did lead thee from one people to another and none would receive thee, Israel alone did welcome thee? And thou, in this nation's time of stress, wilt come up as a witness against her?" These words abashed the Torah and standing aside, she refused to give evidence, so that Abraham was victorious over God. Thereupon God caused the twenty-two letters of the alphabet to endorse Israel's guilt, but Abraham succeeded in turning them also from their purpose. To the Aleph he said, "How comest thou to attest against Israel, thou who art the initial letter of "Anochi Yahwe Elohekha" (I am the Lord thy God), a sentence for which Israel has suffered martyrdom?" Turning to the Beth he said, "Thou art the very first letter of the Torah (Bereshith) which has been exalted by Israel; thou shalt not bear witness against her". Proceeding in this fashion with all the remaining letters, he managed to dissuade them from obeying the command of God to give evidence. Nevertheless God continued to stand firm, and what mere man was unable to effect, was left for the insinuating persuasiveness of a woman to do. Said Rachel, the weeping mother of Israel, to God, "Thou knowest, O Lord, how Thy servant Jacob loved me, and laboured seven years to win me, still when my father substituted my sister for me, I suppressed my grief, nor was I jealous of my sister. How then canst Thou, King of the World, be jealous of so paltry a thing as idolatry and for its sake cause the downfall of Israel?" And God, not failing to be impressed by the delightful boldness of the woman, gave answer, "For thy sake, Rachel, will I forgive them and bring them back to their land" (Midrash Echa Raba).

But more than any other character in the Bible, Moses played the part of a mediator between God and the nation. He was the intercessor to God on Israel's behalf. He invariably sought to alter the divine decisions whenever they meant the punishment of Israel. God Himself was aware of His violent anger, that is why He wept on the day of Moses' death On the angels' asking Him, what was the cause of His weeping, He answered, "Not only for Moses, but for Him and for My children the Jews do I weep. Behold! a queen died and the king lamented: 'Who will now weep for my children, when I, in my exceeding wrath, am about to punish them?' And now the mother of Israel is gone, and no one will be able to restrain My anger, therefore do I weep for him and for the whole of My people" (Vide Byalik an Rawnicki, Sefer ha-Agada, Cracow 5668 Vol. I. p.92) And it was God's own work that Moses died, for when God commanded the archangels Gabriel and Michael to fetch the soul of Moses, they refused to obey the Lord of the Universe "We do not want to steal the soul of Moses, the greatest of men". It was left for the Chief of the Satans, Samael, to go out with his sword against Moses; but even he was forced to retire before the majesty of Moses, and had, perforce, to return to God without having accomplished his object. Moses turned to the sun, the moon, the stars and the rest of nature, and begged them to intercede on his behalf. But from all he received one reply, that they could not pray for him, because they had to pray for themselves, since of every phenomenon in nature it is said in the bible, that they will ultimately perish. There appears in this answer to Moses an embittered protest that death should find place in the world at all. Finally God Himself descended to earth, went to Moses and ordered his soul to leave the body. But the soul emphatically refused to do so "The body of the purest of men I do not wish to leave. Hast Thou found for me a purer and a worthier habitation?" And only when God promised to place her among the Cherubim and the Seraphim, she consented to leave the body of the purest of men. Then God, acting entirely against the wishes of Nature and against the earnest wish of the archangels, touched His servant lightly on the lips and drew forth his soul with a kiss (Idem).

Later on He repented of His act and mourned for the Saviour of Israel.

On one of the occasions when the Children of Israel mutinied against God, who in His anger was about to destroy them, Moses thus interceded for them, "If thou destroyest this people, the nations will say that God was not able to keep His word and that He put to death in the wilderness the people, to whom He had promised freedom. O, let the Might of God show itself great! Pardon the sins of this people!" Commenting on this passage of the Bible, the Talmud says· "Happy is the pupil whose master hearkens to his word" (Berachoth 32).

Even previous to the giving of the Torah on Mount Sinai, Moses had some argument with God. To wit, when Moses ascended to Heaven, he saw, according to a Talmudic version, God inscribing these words in the Tora: "Long-suffering is the Lord". Then asked Moses, "Lord of the Universe, long-suffering surely only to the righteous?" God responded, "Also to the sinners". "Lord", continued Moses, "but didst Thou not say elsewhere, that the transgressors should perish?" And God answered, "There will come a certain day when thou wilt remember our controversy of to-day". And Moses remained silent. But when Israel again sinned (in reference to the Golden Calf) and Moses begged for mercy, God waxed wrathful and said, "Didst thou not once say 'Long-suffering only for the righteous'?" Whereupon Moses said, "But didst Thou not forsooth say 'Also for the sinners'?" (Sanhedrin 111). And in this fashion was God compelled to allow the plea.

Not only does God allow His anger to be easily appeased, but moreover He seeks out those who can help Him to reverse His unpropitious decisions

When He determined to destroy Israel, so relates the Talmud, He turned to Abraham: "Abraham, thy children are transgressing". Abraham said· "Well, let them perish for the sake of Thy Name". Then He turned to Jacob, from whom He received the same reply Thereupon said God, "Not with the hoary head is wisdom and not with the babe is counsel" And, He turned to Isaac: "Isaac, thy children have transgressed." But Isaac said: "Oh Lord, *My* children? Not *Thy* children? When they said, 'We will do and we will listen,' Thou didst call them 'My children,' but now thou sayest 'thy children'? Mine and not Thine? Consider, O Lord, for how long they did sin? Seventy years is the span of life, and only after his twentieth year can a man be held responsible for his own actions, accordingly they could have sinned only fifty years; of these fifty years they sleep twenty five, they pray and eat for another twelve and a half, in which time they cannot sin,—therefore they could only have sinned twelve and a half years out of the seventy. Now, if Thou art able to bear the one half of these sins, then am I prepared to bear the rest, and even if I had to expiate the whole, then I have already done so by my sacrifice" (Sabbath 89). And again had God to concede. Because, after all, He could not but realize, that man, whose heart, created by God, is by Himself described in the Torah as evil from its youth, cannot commit an unexpiable sin. "If I sin, what harm do I to Thee, Thou Guardian of man?" is the grave accusation which Job throws in the face of God. Job does not only put the question "Why is the righteous man unhappy and the wicked happy?", but He puts the much more weighty question "Why should even the wicked man be punished by God?" And even from a less important personage than Job, who was a faithful servant of God, did He receive this challenge, and in far clearer terms, namely from Cain the fratricide. For when God charged him: "Where is thy brother Abel?" he answered, so relates a Midrash, "Am I my brother's keeper? Dost Thou demand an account from *me*? Truly, I demand it from *Thee*, because Thou art the Keeper of all creatures. A robber who stole some valuable vessels by night, was caught by the watchman. The robber complained. "Dost thou abuse me because I stole? Surely, it is thou who shouldst be abused, because it was thy duty to guard and it was for me to steal, because I am a thief." So did Cain address God. "I killed him, but then, Thou didst give me the Evil Impulse (yezer ha-ra); but Thou, Keeper of all creatures, why didst Thou not keep him? Hadst Thou accepted my sacrifice, I would not have been jealous of him and would not have killed him" (Genesis Raba 22).

And God could think of no answer. It is always embarrassing for Him to speak thus "humanly" with His creatures.

From the moment when He revealed the Torah to man, He lost the autocratic powers of an absolute monarch. For the Torah is the constitution which God gave to humanity, and He must observe its statutes as mindfully as His people.

The Torah was according to a tradition drawn up even before the creation of the world, and at the creation, God Himself acted in accordance with it, "as an architect with his plans", to quote the poetical comparison of a Midrash. "So did the Holy One, blessed be His Name, looking in the Torah and creating the world" (Genesis Raba 1).

The Torah, the essence of which is Right and Righteousness, is a supreme law, which stands above God and is, perhaps, to be compared with the Tyche of the Greeks. Just as Tyche was the daughter of Zeus to whom the latter eventually submitted himself, so is the Torah the daughter of God (often actually called in the Talmud by God "My daughter") to whom God submits Himself. But, whereas among the Greeks the Supreme Law becomes finally an attribute of the all-high god Zeus, the law of the Torah, after its revelation to the people, remains independent of God, and is as the layer-down of the law, just as full of authority for Him as for the people. In addition, the nation assumes the right to supervise God's acts, and to demand explanations for any traversities of the law

How narrowly the authority of God is circumscribed can be seen from the following passage of the Talmudic Aggada. While the Rabbis were one day discussing a certain topic in their college, one of the scholars, Rabbi Eliezer, held a view which was not shared by the others. Convinced of the soundness of his opinion Rabbi Eliezer exclaimed, "If I am right, may Heaven confirm it", and a Heavenly Voice (Bath-Kol) was heard: "it is to be decided in favour of Rabbi Eliezer" Thereupon arose Rabbi Josua and said, "She (the Torah) is not in heaven. We do not pay heed to heavenly voices, for Thou, O God, Thyself hast written in Thy Torah 'the majority must prevail', and we, on this side, are in the majority against Rabbi Eliezer". And it was decided against Rabbi Eliezer and the Heavenly Voice. Highly interesting and most beautiful is the remark of the Talmud on this happening. 'On the next day Rabbi Nathan, one of the scholars, encountered the prophet Elijah, of whom he asked, 'What did the Holy One, blessed be His Name, do at that hour?', to which the prophet replied "Laughter was in His voice, and He said 'My children outvoted Me'" (Baba Mezia 59). Here then God stands on an equal footing with the Rabbis. It may be said with much truth that the relationship between God and man is here more intimate than that between father and child. God is at the same time Father and Brother to man. "The Holy One, blessed be His Name, designates the People of Israel brothers, for as it is said 'for the sake of my brothers and friends'; and it is not like brothers who dislike one another, but like Moses and Aaron who loved one another fondly, and exalted one another, and each was happy in the greatness of the other" (Midrash Toledoth Mosche ve-Aharon; Numbers Raba: Exodus Raba 5; Tanchuma Exodus 27).

To our knowledge it is the only place in any religious literature, where the idea of the Brotherhood of God is expressed, an idea which is a great advance on that of the more usual and less daring conception of His Fatherhood.

This courage and grand idea Francesco d'Assisi (12-13. centuries) approached, in that he proclaimed with a deeply felt religious fervour the Brotherhood of Nature When he delivers his famous sermon to the birds addressing them as his "sister-birds," or when he instructs his "sister-turtledoves" to become docile, or when in Rimini he reminds his "brother-fishes" of all the kindnesses shown them by God, or when finally he admonishes his "brother-wolf" to discard his cruelty and to make a covenant of friendship with mankind*, he expresses with a masterful naivity the idea of the Brotherhood of all the creatures of Nature.

In fine this idea breathes through the inimitable "Cantico Del Sole," which E r n e s t R e n a n praises as "le plus beau morceau de poesie religieuse depuis les Evangiles, l'expression la plus complete du sentiment religieux moderne." **

We are at one with the religious feelings of Francesco, when we read his hymn to God, in which he lauds his "*altissimo, onnipotente bon signore*" for all His creations, for the "*messer lo frate Sole*", "*sore luna e le stelle*", "*frate vento*", "*sor acqua*", "*frate foco*". How profound and intimately felt must have been the religion of this poet-preacher, when he calls even death "*sore nostra morte corporale*" and offers thanks to the Creator for this also! A deep thinking mind, and a profoundly feeling soul!

Aptly is it remarked by A d o l f o P a d o v a n in his notes to the abovementioned publication, that we recognise in this psalm the man who loved and exalted the whole Universe, and who lived over twenty years in a "holy communion with nature." ("*Si riconosce in questo salmo l'uomo, che amò e esaltò l'Universo mondo, .. che visse più di vent' anni in santa communione con la Natura, nelle grotte, nei forteli, negli eremitaggi*").

And just as the continuous "h o l y c o m m u n i o n w i t h N a t u r e", which was for him in all her manifestations filled with Divinity, has led Francesco to the idea of B r o t h e r h o o d o f

---

* I fioretti di San Francesco e il Cantico Del Sole, Milano 1915. pp. 47, 69, 121, 66
** Nauvelles etudes d' histoire religieuse, Paris 1884.

N a t u r e, the Rabbis, soaking themselves in reflexions on the Essence of God, arrived by their continuous "h o l y c o m m u n i o n w i t h G o d," at the idea of the B r o t h e r h o o d o f G o d To this conception the hermit of Assisi could not rise. And as for him the earth is both nourishing mother and sister begotten by the same Father ("*soia nosha madre terra*"), so is God for the Rabbis of the above mentioned Midrash the Father, to whom they draw near with devoted prayers and childlike veneration, and a Brother, to whom they feel more akin and trustful.

As an elder Brother He rejoices over the development and over the attaining of an independent status by the younger and more helpless brother whom, it is expected of Him, He will cherish. It is superfluous to add that it is the scholars principally, who stand thus intimately with God. Because as it speaks of the upright judge, so it says elsewhere of every scholar, that he, as it were, is a collaborator in the creation of the world (Seder Arakhim, vide Eisenstein · Ozar Midrashim 70)

In some matters the right to influence the decisions of the scholars is taken away from Him. He is, it is true, the Supreme Judge, and He may give any verdict which to Him appears just, but it is not allowed to Him to fix the day for the considering. and the delivering of the judgement Himself. So much so, that should the whole heavenly host be assembled around the Judgement Seat on the Day of Atonement and the books be ready and open in which it is to be written God's verdict on every single being, nevertheless, if the Rabbis decide upon another day, the proceedings must be postponed. "The Holy One, blessed be His Name, makes a decision and the righteous man waives it aside", which practically amounts to "The righteous man decides and the Holy One, blessed be He, fulfils".

These dicta of the Talmud apply with equal unambiguity in every circumstance. Following on this, every righteous man can, by persistent requests, secure the granting of his wishes, as was the case with Moses who, when he was acquainted with the Divine decision to deliver his soul to the Angel of Death, drew a circle round his feet and addressing himself to God, delivered the ultimatum: "Lord of the Universe! I do not move from here until Thou revokest Thy decision" (Byalik and Rawnicki p.92). God was compelled then to release Moses from the Angel of Death and, as we saw above, Himself to decend to take away his soul.

On another occasion the Angel of Death was not able to carry out his behests simply because the one whom God had decided must die, did not want to die, as we see in the story of the pious and righteous man Ben Sabar. Once the Angel of Death encountered him in the street and told him that he must die. The latter who was still young, prayed to God in the following words: "Lord of the Universe! Shall he who has busied himself with learning and charity die in his youth? Is this the reward for the Torah? Hast Thou decided, that I should die outside my house like a beast of the field?" And God replied: "Time is granted thee until thou wilt go and die in thy bed". Then he departed; on the way he entered the house of the pious and wise man Shfifon and recounted to him his experience. Shfifon tried to console him and when the Angel of Death came to him in his house and said: "I have come to take the lives of both you and Ben Sabar", he made reply: "Go thy way! Thou hast nothing here!" The Angel then betook himself to God and said: "Lord of the Universe! Shfifon bars my entrance". God sent him back and ordered him to tell Shfifon that he wanted only Ben Sabar's life. But when the angel came with this message, Shfifon gave him the same reply as before. At this hour a Heavenly Voice was heard: "What is to be done with these two righteous men? I issue a decree and it cannot be carried out, because it is said 'Thou shalt decree a thing and it shall be established unto thee' (Job 22 28) and it is written 'The righteous man rules the fear of God;'* and who is it that rules over Me? The righteous! For his sake must I revoke My decree!" And God ordered that to each of them seventy years of life should be added (v. Eisenstein Ozar Midrashim p. 334).

Boldness is effective even in Heaven, says a Talmudic proverb (Sanhedrin 105). Following on this the righteous man has for example the power to bring down rain from the heavens simply by an expression of his desire.

Support to this interesting exposition is given by an account of an event appearing in the Annals of the Smithonian Institutions' in Washington (1898), which we were fortunate to see reproduced. In a certain place a long drought prevailed; neither processions nor supplications were of any avail, so that, in desperation, and having lost all patience, the local authorities gave out the following proclamation: "If rain does not fall within a period of eight days, then no man will be obliged to attend divine worship. If another eight days should elapse without rain, then the clergy shall be dismissed and every man shall be permitted to flaunt the commands of God as he listeth." Four days after, so the story runs, strong rains fell.

---

* This is the Talmud's explanation of the very obscure passage II Sam. 23.3 The explanation of the Talmud has it that the righteous man can by his righteousness overcome the decrees of God, which cause fear to any other man (v. Moed Katan 16. Sabbath 53, Baba Mezia 85 Taanith 23, cfr I Kanowitz, The God Idea in Talmud and other Rabbinical Sources, New York 1909, p. 116).

Although this anecdote has its origin in a non-Jewish source, it is worthy of note that it was reprinted in a Jewish journal (Die Welt 1898). The Jewish man-in-the-street would hardly be suprised at the tone of this anecdote. For is he not accustomed since the days of Isaiah to the words of God. "Come, let us reason together"?

Well known are the opening phrases of this piece of declamation of the prophet, so remarkable for its beauty. True, as he continues, he makes God appear as the Victor. "If your sins be as scarlet, shall they be as white as snow? If they be red like crimson, shall they be as wool?" (We consider this to be the only proper translation of the text; cf Gray, and Marti on this point) But the nation has in its bold conviction of its 'having equalled the Most High,' turned the question of the prophet into a definite statement, and almost universally interprets the words of the prophet as "Though your sins be as scarlet, they shall be as white as snow; though they be red like crimson, they shall be as wool"

In Isaiah God wrathful over the sins of Israel emerges victorious; in the later assumption of the people, God is represented as sitting in the Judgment Seat, after He has received the Benediction of Ismael: "May Thy mercy overcome Thine anger!" Mercy, in human estimation, is the supreme virtue which must ennoble God as well as man. Even the most important prohibitions, writing or journeying on the Sabbath, cease to apply to a doctor who must, on his mission of mercy, travel to the sick-bed and write out prescriptions, whenever it may mean the saving of life; but only in that event. Similarly, neither is God Himself permitted to perform any labour on the Sabbath, except it be done for the salvation of life.

This notion found its most untrammeled utterance in a sermon of the celebrated Chassidish Rabbi, Levi Isaac Berditschewer, delivered in the Synagogue on the Day of Atonement, the day when God inscribes in the Book of Life the fate of men. "Lord of the Universe!"—exclaimed the preacher. "It is only allowed according to Thy Holy Commandments, that a doctor should write on the Day of Atonement, when, by so doing, he may be the means of saving a soul; therefore O God, if Thou intendest to save, then affix Thy signature bearing forgiveness to a prosperous year But if Thou meanest to condemn, then I, Levi Isaac, Rabbi of Berditschew, forbid Thee to write on the Day of Atonement".

This Rabbi is generally known as a typical representative of those who stand in the most intimate confidence with God.

It is related of him that once he saw a number of Jews, who for hours endured the pangs of hunger, only because they did not have the water to perform their ablutions, and at the same time, not far away, his eyes fell on a Gentile who, no sooner did he awaken from sleep than he proceeded to eat and drink unconcernedly, and then again lay down to sleep. Struck by the sight, the Rabbi hurried to his Synagogue, flung open the doors of the Holy Ark, and cried out bitterly, "Lord of the Universe! observe well the distinction between the Children of Thy Chosen People and the others! And Thou hast yet grievances against Thy People Israel! And Thou still considerest Thyself justified!"

Again on the Day of Atonement, while preaching, he is reported to have said, "Lord of the Universe! it is incumbent upon Thee to pardon Israel, and if Thou dost it not, then shall I disclose the secret that Thou art crowned with profane phylacteries, God forbid!. Because in Thy phylacteries is written, "Who is like unto Thy People Israel, an only nation on the earth?", and if Thou dost not pardon Israel's sins, they cannot be called 'an only nation'" (Vide Dr. S.A. Horodecki in Miklat 5681, Vol V.p. 264.)

And as the Rabbi of the Chassidim, the Pious (Zadik), as he is cognomened by the nation, decided, so God—volens nolens— had to admit and to pardon.

On another occasion when this Rabbi had reason to think that God was dissatisfied with his prayers, he became decidedly vexed with Him. On the festival of New-Year it was customary with him to blow the Shofar. In his girdle were stuck a number of Shofroth. On this particular occasion he attempted as usual to blow, but although he tried each Shofar in return, not one would emit a single note. Such a thing can only happen, according to popular belief, if the blower be an impious man and Satan stand before him, or if the congregation be sinful. The Rabbi growing furious, threw down his Shofar, and cried out, "Well then! let Ivan blow the Shofar!" (Ivan was the name of the Gentile Sabbath servant).

"If thou wilt bring an unmerciful verdict, shall we, the righteous and pious of this generation, proceed to nullify that verdict?" runs another saying of this Rabbi.

Chassidism, a Jewish mystical movement which arose in the 18th century, has manifestly subjected the actions of God to the decisions of its Rabbis to whom, having honoured them with the appelation 'Righteous' they apply the Talmudic saying, "The righteous man decides, and the Holy One, blessed be He, effects".

The Rabbis of the Chassidim took the liberty of even sitting in judgment upon God; and time and again were they invoked by individuals with grievances against Him.

Once a Chassid brought the following well-founded plea against God. "The Talmud tells us, that when a slave who serves two masters at the same time, is freed by the one and not by the other, he is half free and half slave. It is permitted to him to marry neither a slave-woman on account of his semi-freedom, nor a free-woman on account of his semi-thraldom. How then may he be enabled to fulfil the duty of becoming married? The second master is then obliged also to set him at liberty in order that he may marry a free woman. Now, O Rabbi! My daughter is like myself free, but she is a slave to Poverty, who does not want to free her, therefore she is unable to marry, because no one desires to wed a poor slave of need. The one who is alone Master of Wealth and Poverty is God; therefore He alone can be regarded in the light of the second master who has in his hands the power to set my daughter at full liberty. And according to the previously mentioned passage in the Talmud, He must do it." The Rabbis could not but give the verdict in the plaintiff's favour; and God, acquiescing in the finding, caused the daughter in the course of the year to become rich, and thus enabled her to marry.

"Boldness is effective even in heaven". One need only understand how to force the issue as Jacob did.

In a similar manner was God embarassed by another Chassid. It was in a Rumanian village. The Hospodar of the village inflicted a pernicious law on the Jews. What was to be done? A devout Chassid, by name Feiwel, discovered that the law was in conflict with the behests of God. Accordingly he hastened to the Rabbi and said in the presence of him and two other Rabbis: "I desire to have a suit with God. The law of the Hospodar is a violation of the Torah. In the Torah it is stated that we are God's servants and only He is our master, wherefore He alone has the right to punish us, because according to the Divine Law one man has not the right to punish the servant of another. Since we have mutually agreed to carry out the Torah, this law applies with as much force to God as to us. Consequently God is compelled to render null and void the law of the hospodar''. And the Rabbi said: "Among us it is a rule, that after the case has been presented by both parties, both of them must leave the Chamber. Feiwel should therefore go away. But as the departure of God is neither to be desired nor possible, because He is Omnipresent and without Him we cannot exist an hour, it would be an injustice to make an exception for Him and to allow Him alone to remain. Therefore Feiwel may also remain" And the Rabbis consulted the law-books and found that God was entirely in the wrong in allowing the Hospodar to promulgate laws against Israel, and they upheld Feiwel's objections, "a servant may not be chastised by any but his own master". Three brought in and endorsed the verdict, and God, as One, had to bow to the judgment which had been given by the three

Three days later, it is said, the troublsome law was repealed.

Here also God was outvoted, and even if He had had something to suggest, He would have had one vote as against three; and this was only what He had Himself laid down, for did He not state in the Torah: "Hear, O Israel, the Lord is *One*"?

But the unity is not the only characteristic which often brings God into difficulties He is also Holy, Kadosh, that is literally 'gathered, fully prepared, morally perfect'. It is by reason of this perfection that He stands over and above man. Man will ever be unable to attain the state the Bible pictures: "Be Holy, for the Lord thy God is Holy", but at the most by a constant striving may approach the fulfilment of that blessed condition. In this striving, man is to be aided by God, Who, by opening to his gaze the vista of a moral life in the revealed Torah and also by the assumption of the responsibility to assure his material well-being, and thus absolving him from mundane cares, has it in his power to give him the opportunity to live a divinely moral life "Wherever I record My Name I shall come to thee and bless thee". This undertaking He is obliged to honour. But if He fails to do so, then it is not for Him to find fault with a Job, should he be ensnared in the meshes of Satan. Surely only if He carries out His part of the agreement can He be justified in demanding of the soul who stands at the portals of Heaven "Hast thou been honest in thine earthly deeds?" (Im nassata wenathata beemuna?")

A certain Jew who was once thus challenged, answered the Lord of the Universe: "And Thou, O Lord, hast Thou dealt honourably with Thy People?" "What wrong then have I done?" asked God of him, and the Jew replied· "That would I not say, because Thou wouldst then have to be ashamed". But on God's loudly exclaiming, "I order thee to speak," the Jew said. "Thy command must I obey. Hearken then: The Jews, who serve Thee faithfully and adore Thee alone, go through life in abject poverty; but the Christians who assign to Thee a wife and a son, enjoy wealth and even luxury. And I am a poor Jew. Is it to be wondered at, that I should now and then be led to do unworthy acts in my affairs? Why dost Thou not have a care for my well-fare as Thou didst promise? I should like to see what would be Thy course, If Thou wert in reality burdened with a wife and children and had a God who cared for Thee as Thou carest for us". And there was silence on the part of the Lord of the

Universe. Perhaps, as the result of the unbridled speech of this Jew, He had realised for the first time, how difficult it often is for men to tread the narrow path of duty "If Thou wert a man, and wert Thyself to experience human suffering, Thou wouldst be more gentle in Thy treatment," is the inner meaning of this Jew's complaint.

The thought is old and genuinely characteristic of the Jewish folk-soul, lying as it does at the root of one of the most powerful creations of the Jewish mentality, namely at that of Christianity.

To remind God of His promises, to admonish Him to fulfil His duties is considered by the Jew as absolutely within His rights Often he takes the liberty to criticise God's commands and actions from a standpoint of purely human reason

Referring to the Divine Command forbidding the eating of the fruit of the Tree of Wisdom, the Zohar says, that, since the command is given in the words " Lo thokhal mimmennu " being the masculine, singular, imperative form, it was meant to apply to Adam alone, more especially in view of the fact that Eve was according to the version in the second chapter of Genesis created subsequently, and therefore was perfectly innocent of eating the fruit, and God was wrong in condemning her.*

This decision of the Zohar was of course post factum, so that God could not recall the undeserved condemnation of Eve. Modern women have to regret that Eve was not better versed in Hebrew grammar, otherwise perhaps, she would have been in a position to find a suitable excuse and God would have accepted her contention as later on He accepted the contention of her descendant Rachel, for whose sake He revoked the decision to destroy the nation

*According to verbal information from Dr S A Horodecki

Another example is known to us of a woman who knew how, by clever ruse, to influence God and by this means to save her husband from death In the Midrash Decalogue which was compiled about the 10th century, the following story is told in connection with a reflection on the seventh commandment.

The good and pious Rabbi Reuben who had always had the power of annuling through his prayers harmful decrees against the Jews, had one son. Once the Angel of Death informed him in confidence, that his son must die. The pious father did not dare to murmer against the decision of God, but he asked the angel to stay his hand until the son should become married. The Angel of Death, who often appears in Jewish folk-lore if not altogether as a *sora morte*, at least as a friendly spirit, conceded this request. But on the wedding-day he appeared before the young bridegroom and revealing to him who he was he declared that he had come to fetch his soul. The young man asked for permission to kiss his bride once more before he died. Obtaining this permission, he brought the mournful news to the bride, but she did not show the least inclination to yield. Approaching the Angel she asked him : " Sire, didst thou come for the soul of my husband ? He said: "Yes ! " She said: "Thus it is written in the Torah : When a man hath taken a new wife, he shall be free at home one year, and shall cheer up his wife which he has taken " (Deut. 24. 5.) The Angel said : " Wait until I return to the Holy One, blessed be He, perhaps He will do this for the sake of His Name and will have pity on you." And when he appeared before God's Throne he found the Archangels there beseeching God to show mercy to Rabbi Reuben. But their prayers seemed to him of little avail. Then he said to God : " Lord of the Universe ! Thus and thus the woman said !" "And forthwith," the story ends, " God was filled with pity and he granted the condemned man seventy more years of life corresponding to the seven wedding days, to carry out the words of the Holy writ · " He will fulfil the desire of them that fear Him " (Ps. 145 9.) God had to concede because He could not act contrary to the words of His own Law.

From olden times innumerable similar stories have come to us in manuscripts and books. In modern times they are to be found in the oral folk-traditions which very often have their origin in the distant past

The bringing into question of God's words and works looms largely in modern Jewish folk-lore.

The celebrated preacher of Chelm is reported to have narrated the following story during the course of a sermon preached in a small village where the moral tone does not appear to have been very high. " I was wandering in the fields where I met the Almighty, so I said to Him, " Good morning, Almighty," and He returned the greeting, " Good morning, dear Magid of Chelm." So I said, " Almighty, Almighty, I would ask Thee a question." And He : " Ask, Magid of Chelm, and I will answer " I said : " Almighty, Almighty ! Thou hast given us a precious Torah, Thou hast said in Thy Torah, " Thou shalt not murder," and this without a doubt is right. How dost Thou mean murder ? How can Jews come to murder ? And further Thou hast told us, " Thou shalt not steal;" also right! Stealing! But further Thou hast told us, " Thou shalt not commit adultery." Now I ask of Thee, what has that to do with Thee? What hast Thou to do with other people's business? And he answered me: " Thou art right, Magid of Chelm ! I should indeed have not written it , but it is now done, and the Torah may not be altered, so I beg of thee, tell it to nobody, let it remain a secret between Me and thee." Now I ask ye, my brethren, how can it remain a secret between me and the Almighty, when every young wife in your small village already knows this secret?"

Such unexpected turns which offend or unmask others or disclose their weaknesses, exercise a strong appeal for the common people. This preference is also to be discerned in the following story which contains traces of a contention with God. A Lithuanian Jew once narrated to another Jew who was a warden in an American Synagogue, the following: A bastard once complained to God: "Why didst Thou lay punishment on me in the Torah? In what am I to blame? Thou shouldst have punished my parents, not me" God said· "Rest tranquil; true, thou art despised and persecuted, nobody wishes to have anything to do with thee; but, a time will come when thou wilt go to America and there thou wilt become a warden"

Often besides God's words His actions are brought to account. "God took from me 10,000 roubles and then—my wife" complained a Jew against God before a Rabbi. "How unjust! how unreasonable! One would not have expected such a deed of God; much rather, He should have first taken my wife, the 10,000 roubles afterwards; for then I had got me a new wife with another 10,000 roubles as dowry; and then both God and I would have each a wife and each 10,000 roubles." The story goes no further. But if the Rabbi did decide; then God would have surely been obliged to return the money

God often has it very hard with His Chosen People. He frequently falls into a passion with His children, but he allows His anger to be readily assuaged. "Were God not to take a jest in good part"—aye, then would the gates of Heaven be closed not to

Luther alone. He does not take amiss these escapades of His chil-, dren. One with whom God was exceedingly angry went, so it is, told, on the Day of Atonement to the woods, drew surreptitiously a flask of brandy from his pocket, and calledout : " Lechaim, Gott ! Good-health, O Lord ! Once Thou didst play me a joke in that, Thou didst not keep to Thy word and allowed me to become poor. , Very well then, now it is my turn to play a joke, and I also will circumvent my promise 'We will do and listen,' by drinking brandy to-day. So shall we be annoyed with each other? But listen further, I will again drink, 'good-health O Lord,' and we will make it up again "

In Jewish folk-lore we often meet with such a familiar tone in the Techinoth (prayer-books) of the women, in popular tales and jokes, no would anyone who is-well acquainted with the true character of the nation see in this familiarity a travesty of religious feelings. But on the other hand it denotes so intense a religious conviction as to lead a Jewess, whose daughter lay ill, to run into the Synagogue, and having wrenched open the Holy Ark, cry out, "Lord of the Universe ! If Thou wilt heal my daughter, it shall be well , and if not, then Thou must know that I shall go away to my sister!" She did not doubt that God, Who loved her personally, desired also her personal love, and would be unwilling to give her cause to become annoyed with Him. In the same way the Jew was convinced that He would accept his "Lechaim."

Once on a Day of Atonement (on which the Divine Service lasts the whole day) a poor Jewish woman is said to have remark-, ed. "I know that I have committed many sins, but God will surely have pity on me and forgive me." On people asking her, why she was so sure about it, she answered: "Would not even a murderer have pity on anyone who prayed to him for twenty-four hours?"

And God the Omnipotent will surly become reconciled with the wretched sinners. He is the God of forgiveness and mercy. Even when he sees that men are guilty, His infinite Love does not allow him to punish them. This thought is quaintly expressed in the following passage of the Talmud. Said Rabbi Yuda: "Of twelve hours does the day consist. The first three hours the Holy One, blessed be He, is studying the Torah. The following three He judges the whole world. And as He sees that all the world is sinful and guilty of condemnation, He leaves the throne of judgment and occupies the throne of Mercy?" (Abhodah Zarah 2.)

After all it was He Himself Who said, "I do not want the death of the sinner, but that he should abandon sin, and live." To abolish the need of material things which alone causes sin, is therefore more the concern of God then of men, because when man sins, that which suffers first is the Glory of God. In a world, in the realm of which God styles Himself King, He as King should have the ability to establish Right and Righteousness. It is for him to see that the Torah, the "Purity" (Reinigkeit), as it is popularly termed, permeates life with absolute purity. If He does not do it, it is an admission of His weakness.

Wolwel Ehrenkranz adopted this thought as the theme of one of his celebrated folk-melodies. A poor pedlar seeking a livlihood for himself and his wife and twelve children, bitterly bewailed his lot: that he cannot pray, that he cannot, though he would, carry out the requirements of religion while necessity and want oppressed him. After much shedding of tears and reproachs against Heaven, he cried out in his anguish:

> My mind is at a standstill now,
> Enough of lamenting and weeping!
> Let the Lord now do what He will,
> The world is surely His, not mine!

In the next world, which is God's world *kat eroihen* there awaits the Jew who strives after uprightness full recompense for all the hardships and weeping of his sojourn on earth. For God has pledged to every righteous man in the Hereafter three hundred and ten worlds which will be placed at his complete disposal. Another poem of the same poet picturesquely describes the distribution of these worlds.

Before God's Throne winds a procession of pious souls demanding their rewards The Almighty finds himself in a serious predicament, and he seeks to satisfy their clamouring with temporary consolation prizes. But when the crowd turbulently insists on the immediate distribution of the promised worlds, He appeals to it thus:

> , How can I "—says He—"still your just demands?
> Truly I am the mighty God,
> But whence to take so many worlds?"
> And He declared Himself bankrupt!

But also to those who are still alive, does God owe a debt which he should have long ago discharged.

It is the vow to make the People as the sand on the seashore and as the stars in the sky. "Sand and Stars" the well-known poem of F r u g terminates with the following powerful stanza of despairing reproach against God.

Yes, God dear (Gotenju), true, as the sands and the stones
Scattered and splintered, trodden under foot.
But of the stars, resplendent and twinkling ?
O, the stars, where are the stars, O God ?

Just as the nation holds controversy with her God, so she causes other people to strive with theirs, but as is apparent in the following example in quite a different strain.

A Polish Shlachtits (Squire) was accustomed, so it is related amongst Jews, to come to the church every day at the same hour and to pray, "O Lord Jesus ! Grant me an estate and a thousand roubles." Day in, day out was heard the same prayer. Finally the sexton of the church losing patience ascended to the gallery and when the Shlachtits had recited his usual prayer, he cried out, "Nie dam ! I will not give ! " Then screamed he Shlachtits furiously, "Yak nie dash ? What dost thou mean, Thou wilt not give ? I am a Polish Shlachtits, and Thou art merely a Jew óf Bethlehem ! "

Cognate with the theme of a dispute with God is the theme of a dispute on God's behalf, which similarly finds its origin in the documents of Jewish antiquity, plays an important role in the Talmudic Aggada and is an effective element in modern Jewish folk-lore. Two examples of this subject may be here permitted for the sake of completeness.

Said an Emperor to Rabban Gamliel: Your God is a thief, because it is said: "And the Lord God caused a deep sleep to fall upon Adam, and he slept . and he took one of his ribs." Said his daughter to Rabban Gamliel "Leave him to me, I shall answer him." And she spoke to the emperor . " Give me a duke "* He asked: " For what do you need one ?" She replied : " Robbers came this night into my house : they stole a

---

* Duke (dukas) in talmudic language means a military or a police efficer.

silvern vessel and have left a golden one in its place." He spoke to her:. "May such robbers come to us every day." Then she said: "And was it not good for Adam, that one rib was taken from him and he was given a wife in its place?" (Sanh. 39.)

And so the daughter of Rabban Gamliel quashed the accusation of the emperor.

Another example of this kind of discussion may be taken from modern Jewish folk-lore.

A priest in conversation with a Rabbi, a friend of his, said, " I have a strong liking and respect for the Jewish Faith, but one thing grieves me. Why do you persist in believing in a God of Vengeance? Why do you not rather accept our God of Love? Is not the conception of the God of Vengeance lower than our creed? The Rabbi answered, "I do not dispute it, certainly our God is a God of Vengeance, and yours a God of Love; but what is to be understood under the term " God of Vengeance"? It means, He is the God of Vengeance, we cede to Him all Vengeance and we practise love. If now, with you. Christians the roles are reversed, we certainly are not to be blamed." This of course is jest. But is it not the only proper answer to a so oft heard question which can itself only be taken up as a jest? In fact, no adequate expression for God's Essence can be found in definitions of human language. God of Love? God of Vengeance? How can our human mind presume to translate human traits and human virtues to Him, he Infinite? For all eternity will it remain the highest endeavour of religious thought to try to comprehend God with perfect clearness. It matters little how we name Him, but rather how He permeates our life. And in this respect, I believe, that the religion of everyone of us, in so far as it is not a rote-learned dogma, but a genuine experience of God, unravebly knotted with all our virtues and vices, passions and meditations, can be called Henotheism. Max Mueller coined this term to describe the specific form of Vedic religion. "This is the peculiar character of the ancient Vedic religion, which I have tried to characterise as Henotheism or Kathenotheism, a successive belief in single supreme gods, in order to keep it distinct from that phase of religious thought which we comonly call Polytheism, in which the many gods are already subordinated to one supreme god, and by which therefore the craving after the One without a second has been more fully satisfied. In the Veda one God after another is invoked. For the time being, all that can be said of a divine being, is ascribed to him. The poet while adddesssing him, seems hardly to know about any other gods. But in the same collection of hymns, sometime even in the same hymn, other gods are mentioned and they also are truly divine, truly ndependent, or, it may be, supreme. The vision of the worshipper seems to change suddenly, and the same poet who at one moment saw nothing but the sun as ruler of heaven and earth, now sees heaven and earth as the father and mother of the sun and of all the gods." (Lectures on the Origin and Growth of Religion, as illustrated by the religions of India, Page 271, London 1880). The Henotheism is consequently a monotheistic system, in which now one, now another of the gods is *the* God. If we substitute in the place of the single gods, the attributes that we ascribe to God, we will clearly recognise Henotheism in ourselves. If we, as religious men, are called upon to bear a great affliction and we feel the need of the help of the Almighty, then we bow our heads or clasp our hands and we pray to God, who is for us in this mood of our souls the All-Loving. At that moment we think only of His goodness and love, and the thought that He is also a strong and punishing judge, does not enter our mind. But when in another mood of our spirit we think of the wrong done to us by others, when we feel offence and anger,—a natural feeling which cannot be hypocritically dogmatised away,—and we are religious, that is, bound to God in every agitation of our mind, then we look to heaven and we pray to God to defend our honour and fortune and to punish those who have wronged us Here we forget altogether that on a former occasion we ourselves appealed to quite another quality of God As long as we mortals live as we do to-day, we shall remain Henothesists.

Only after every oppression, every persecution, and as a consequence, every hatred and revenge will have been expurged from human life, will vanish from our mind the idea of an avenging God. This is the time of the future, prophesied by Isaiah, when the lion and the lamb shall graze together. The Jew calls that time " the day of the eternal Sabbath."

It is believed that on the Sabbath there enters the breast of the Jew a higher soul (neshama jethera), which is entirely devoted to holiness. But as the Sabbath expires, the Jew recites the Havdala-prayer, in which he praises God, Who has distinguished the Sabbath from the other days. Then the higher soul leaves him and the every-day soul re-enters his breast.

The great poet J. L Peretz in his drama "The Golden Chain" painted powerfully the longing of the Jew after the Eternal Sabbath It is in this drama, where the theme of the contention with God, familiar to us through Jewish folk-lore, has found its highest artistic conception

Supported by the belief that before the Sabbath can come to a close, the Chassidic Rabbi must recite the Havdala, Rabbi Shelomo, the chief of the Chassidim, desiring to hold the Sabbath for ever, refuses to recite it. The heavens show with heavy clouds and snow storm their anger at the proud and presumptious resolution of the Rabbi. The whole town demands of him to retract and, in fine, to fulfil the manifested will of heaven. But he remains strongly by his resolve: "Shelomo does not recite the Havdala." The Jews could not therefore reopen their shops and resume their ordinary activities. Timourously they ask the Rabbi: "What shall become of it? Shall the world be destroyed? And then, "yes indeed," he cried out, "this world, let it be destroyed! And we Jews exalted by the Sabbath glory, inspired by our higher soul, Jews of festival spirit, shall march over her ruins! Let the Sabbath not cease to be! Singing and dancing we shall go to Him, we shall stand before God's throne! O, we do not pray, we do not beg; we say to him, "Longer we could not wait! The Song of Songs we sing! Singing and dancing we go!" Thus he wanted to hold fast the Sabbath on earth, to expunge the every day from life, and to put an end even to the suffering in hell, because according to the folk-belief, the doomed in hell too, enjoy respite on the Sabbath He remained firm, convinced that God would yield to his decision. But at this moment, in the midst of the most exalted inspiration of the Rabbi, a Jew enters the room and calls out to those present the every day greeting "Gutt Woch!" (good week). A son of the Rabbi had had the audacity to recite the Havadala in spite of his father, whose prerogative he had dared to assume. And thus the spell was broken. "They did not allow", the aged Rabbi sighed. He did not outlive the great pain of his religious disappointment.

Ages will pass, but yet in the end this longing for the eternal Sabbath will have to conquer the soul of every human being. Then will humanity, in common resolve establish a life in which even work, hard work, all that to-day is every-day sorrow, will be pure, noble and holy. In that time of Eternal Sabbath no longer shall we seek definitions of God, for He Himself in His shining light will live in the hearts and spirits of all the sons of men.

It would be superfluous to emphasise that the religiousness of the Jew should not appear less by reason of his presumption to criticise God, to remonstrate with Him, to admonish Him, and to indict him before the Supreme Law, the Torah. But rather, in these passages of arms with God are expressed the depths of religious sentiment. The Jewish nation is according to the words of her prophets, a Servant of God (Ebed Yahweh); but God is not Lord and Master, but Father, Husband and Brother, Who requires the aid of the servant for the carrying out of Divine plans.

Israel, the Servant of God, precociously imagines herself a part of God. Such conception could well-nigh be termed "megalomania of a crowd." But it is not megalomania when the Ebed Yahweh is actively aware of the distinction which this servitude confers and of the responsibility which it places on him The formula "God, Israel, and the Torah form a unity" was the source of this conviction.

In the various aspects of the contention with God is to be traced the battle to acquire this unity, 'the sainted longing' *His* (Selige Sehnsucht.) of the nation after a 'Higher Betrothal."

It is in the nature of things that the struggle assumes various forms according to the stages of the spiritual development of the people.

Everybody is "like the Spirit whom he comprehends.' The Shechinah, the Soul of God, is for the people that Spirit Whom it comprehends and Whom she considers herself like.

The higher the development of the mind, the wider is its conception of God. But however highly developed one's mind may be, one's image of God can never coincide with His real Essence. Every image of God, arising from logical conclusions or merely sentimental motives, will always contain a trace of 'weakness in strength.' But when we find ourselves in the bosom of nature and we merge ourselves wholly in her so that we cease to exist separately from her, when the flood of our thoughts and the impetuous waves of our sentiments flow together into that wide, calm, translucent sea which we call Soul, when this soul draws into itself simultaneously all the majestic rays and sents and melodies of nature,—then it becomes unified with·Him, the Soul of the Universe. And thus it is said in the Talmud :

King David praised God with the words "Bless the Lord, O my Soul" (Ps. 103). Just as none knows the place of the soul so none knows the place of God; may then the soul, whose place we do not know, come to praise God, Who is exalted over His world and Whose place we do not know And as the Holy One fills the Universe, so the soul fills the body ; as He sees and is not to be seen, so the soul, who sees, cannot be seen ; as He sustains the world, so the soul sustains the body ; as He is pure, so is the soul pure ; as He is hidden, so is the soul hidden ;   may therefore the soul, distinguished by these five attributes, bless God, Who is distinguished by the same five attributes, " Bless the Lord, O my Soul " (Sanh. 39 ; Berakhoth 10.) *

The Soul of the individual blesses the Soul of the Universe! Before Him, the Soul of the Universe, our speech remains dumb.

That Spirit, which we cannot be like, because we cannot comprehend it, the All-Embracer, about Whom we do not dare to assert " He is " or " He is not," the All-Sustainer, Who shines in the tranquil glow of the rays of the rising sun, Who glitters in the " starry sky above us," Who looks at us through the shining eyes of our children, and Who pervades everything that has life or is life giving,—of Him, Whose Hand we perceive at work in ourselves with a child-like happy astonishment, we say at every time and in every place, " Holy, Holy, Holy is the Lord of the Hosts, the Fulness of the World is His Glory "

————o————

* Similarly and pe: aps under the Influence of this passage of the Talmud, the author of the anonymous treatise "De Anima " which has been falsely attributed to Hugh of St Victor, wrote in the 13th chapter of the 2nd Book of this treatise "Habet quoque anima vires, quibus corpori commiscetur Quarum prima est naturalis secunda vitalis tertia animalis Et sicut deus trinus et unus et perfectus omnia tenet omnia implet omnia superexcedit et circumplecitur sic anima Cfr Giovanni Melodia La Vita Nuova di Dante Alighieri, Milano 1911, p. 12, note 12,

BM
530
O4

THE LIBRARY
UNIVERSITY OF CALIFORNIA
Santa Barbara

STACK COLLECTION

THIS BOOK IS DUE ON THE LAST DATE STAMPED BELOW.

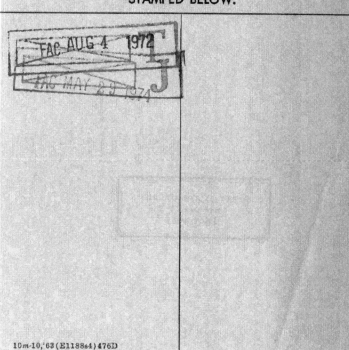

FAC AUG 4 1972

FAC MAY 29 1974

10m-10,'63(E1188s4)476D